What Is an Election?

Sherry Howard, M.Ed.

Reader Consultants

Cheryl Norman Lane, M.A.Ed.
Classroom Teacher
Chino Valley Unified School District

Jennifer M. Lopez, M.S.Ed., NBCT
Teacher Specialist—History/Social Studies
Norfolk Public Schools

iCivics Consultants

Emma Humphries, Ph.D.
Chief Education Officer

Taylor Davis, M.T.
Director of Curriculum and Content

Natacha Scott, MAT
Director of Educator Engagement

Publishing Credits

Rachelle Cracchiolo, M.S.Ed., *Publisher*
Emily R. Smith, M.A.Ed., *VP of Content Development*
Véronique Bos, *Creative Director*
Dona Herweck Rice, *Senior Content Manager*
Dani Neiley, *Associate Content Specialist*
Fabiola Sepulveda, *Series Designer*

Image Credits: p.11 Jake Lyell/Alamy; p.15 The George W. Bush Presidential Library; p.17 (left) Library of Congress; p.17 (right) Smith Collection/Gado/Getty Images; p.18 Alexander Drago/Reuters/Newscom; p.19 Brittany Murray/MediaNews Group/Long Beach Press-Telegram via Getty Images; p.20 Library of Congress [LC-USZ62-59401]; p.25 (top) UPI / Alamy Stock Photo; p.25 (bottom) UPI/Newscom; p.27 Bettmann/Getty Images; p.29 (bottom) Jeff Malet Photography/Newscom; all other images from iStock and/or Shutterstock.

Library of Congress Cataloging-in-Publication Data

Names: Howard, Sherry, author.
Title: What is an election? / Sherry Howard, M.Ed.
Description: Huntington Beach, CA : Teacher Created Materials, [2021] |
  Includes index. | Audience: Grades 2-3 | Summary: "In the United States,
  government leaders are elected. The highest leader in the nation is the
  president. Every four years, voters choose who the next president will
  be. But the road to the White House begins long before Election Day and
  involves lots of people. Learn more about the process of electing
  government leaders"-- Provided by publisher.
Identifiers: LCCN 2020016209 (print) | LCCN 2020016210 (ebook) | ISBN
  9781087605104 (paperback) | ISBN 9781087619293 (ebook)
Subjects: LCSH: Elections--United States--Juvenile literature. |
  Voting--United States--Juvenile literature.
Classification: LCC JK1978 .H69 2021 (print) | LCC JK1978 (ebook) | DDC
  324.60973--dc23
LC record available at https://lccn.loc.gov/2020016209
LC ebook record available at https://lccn.loc.gov/2020016210

This book may not be reproduced or distributed in any
way without prior written consent from the publisher.

5482 Argosy Avenue
Huntington Beach, CA 92649-1039
www.tcmpub.com

ISBN 978-1-0876-0510-4
© 2022 Teacher Created Materials, Inc.

The name "iCivics" and the iCivics logo are
registered trademarks of iCivics, Inc.
Printed in China
WaiMan

Table of Contents

Leaders in Our World.................................. 4

Jump into Fiction:
    Vote Katy!.. 6

Group Leaders 10

Campaigns and Elections 16

Election Day.. 26

Staying Involved 28

Glossary... 30

Index.. 31

Civics in Action..................................... 32

Leaders in Our World

In every family, there is a leader or two. Who that leader is changes for each family. Family leaders are meant to take care of everyone. They make sure their families have what they need.

Schools have leaders too. Most school leaders are adults. But students can lead as well. Some students act as safety patrols. Others serve on student councils. These leaders do what they can to make sure schools and students have what they need.

U.S. government
leaders help a city.

People **elect** the leaders in government. They choose
them by voting. The leaders may work for cities, counties,
or states. Some, such as the president, work for the nation.
National leaders make sure the country has what it needs.

Jump into
Fiction

Vote Katy!

It was time for a new student council. Katy wanted to be president of the council, but she had to get elected first. She decided to make posters for her campaign. Katy loved posters!

One thing Katy didn't love was public speaking. And for this election, she would have to give a speech. She'd have to stand in front of the whole school. What did people want from their president?

"What can student council do better?" Katy asked over and over. She asked students. She asked teachers. She even asked Mr. Knots, the principal.

Everybody wanted something different. Teachers wanted students to work hard and have fun while they learned. Students wanted longer recesses. Mr. Knots wanted people to keep the school clean! On one issue, teachers and kids agreed. They wanted new grass for the playing fields.

Katy knew what to say. She got busy writing.

Speech day arrived at last. Mr. Knots spoke first. "Remember to think about what people say they will do for the school," he said. "Can the candidates keep their promises? Do they have the power to do the things they say they will?"

Juan was the first candidate. "We need longer recess," he said. "Vote for me, and I'll make sure you have more time to play!" He also promised ice cream with lunch once a week. More and more candidates spoke. They all promised fun things. Katy wondered if they could keep their promises.

Finally, Katy's turn came. She took a deep breath. "We need new grass for our playing fields," she began. "The grass we have now is dead. When the wind blows, it picks up a lot of dirt. It is not safe for us. Mr. Knots has approved this change." Everyone clapped—they thought it was a good idea!

After the speeches, students cast their votes. Mr. Knots counted them. Katy won the election! The students liked that she made a promise she could keep.

Back to Nonfiction

Group Leaders

Some leaders are elected and some are not. Katy was elected to the student council. Her speech convinced people to vote for her. Families have leaders too. People don't elect family leaders. But most of us agree on who our family leader is.

Some leaders are **appointed**. For example, a classroom might have a line leader. The line leader is appointed by the teacher to get the line of students where they need to go.

People live in communities, which are small groups. Some communities have elected leaders and some don't. These leaders might be mayors or council members.

The bigger the group, the more likely there will be an elected leader instead of an appointed leader. When someone is elected, everyone has a say in who their leader is.

This man is a leader in his community.

Think and Talk

Who are the leaders in your life?
How do they lead?

Our country has groups of all sizes in it. Some groups may find it hard to work together. The bigger the group, the harder it can be. People may disagree on important things. And it can be hard to get people to agree.

That is why large groups need leaders. Leaders help people work together to find the common good for the group. Once the group agrees on how to move forward, they can make progress.

Elected leaders make sure **services**, such as fire departments, are paid for.

This mayor helps plant trees in a town park.

A city is a type of large group. Cities need things such as roads and schools. They also need access to water, healthcare, and other services. Elected city leaders make sure these needs are met. For instance, maybe a city needs a new bridge, but people can't agree on where it should be built. A good leader will work hard to help the group find the best location.

Voters try to elect leaders who will make good decisions. Voters depend on their leaders to help them. Leaders depend on voters to keep them in **office**.

Just as people in a city need to work together, so do people in counties and states. All these places combine to form the nation. People who work in the **federal** government provide a lot of services. They make sure people get their mail. They decide how to spend the country's money. They work to protect us. They do many other helpful things too. They can do all these things because there are lots of strong leaders working together.

The federal government controls the postal service.

Former President George W. Bush meets with other government leaders.

The United States' highest leader is the president. Their job is to represent the needs and wants of the whole nation. Not everyone will be happy with the president all the time. But the president works with other parts of the government to try to make the best decisions for everyone.

In the United States, people elect the nation's leaders. The United States is a **representative democracy**. This means that **citizens** choose the leaders they think will do the best job. You may not be able to vote yet. But you can still learn about who is running for office.

Greek Roots

The United States is a democracy. The word *democracy* comes from two Greek words—*dēmos* and *kratos*. *Dēmos* means "common people." *Kratos* means "rule" or "strength." So, in a democracy, the people have the power.

Campaigns and Elections

Every four years, Americans elect a president in November. But the process often starts years earlier. **Candidates** spend hundreds of millions of dollars to get elected. They pay for ads on TV. They travel around the country hosting events and meeting voters. They make signs that people put in their yards. Voters can feel overwhelmed by the number of candidates. It can be hard to know the best person to elect.

Learning about candidates takes a long time. People sometimes go to hear candidates speak. People read about candidates online. Candidates make a lot of promises and talk about their plans. Voters have to decide whether they agree with those plans.

Each **campaign** will have a strong message. A message is a quick way of saying what they think is most important. Voters can tell a lot about candidates from their messages. Candidates spread their messages as much as they can. Candidates' messages are repeated over and over again until the election.

A Successful Slogan

Campaign messages are often in the form of brief **slogans** or sayings. President Dwight "Ike" Eisenhower had a famous one. It was simply "I like Ike." His campaign was the first to focus on using TV to reach voters.

Campaign Committees

Candidates can't win elections on their own. They need help for that! Candidates build campaign committees. These are groups of people who all want the same person to win the election. They work as a team. Their goal is to have their candidate elected.

Some people on a campaign committee are paid for their work. Others volunteer their time for free. They see it as part of their **civic duty**.

Campaign volunteers prepare materials to support their candidate.

Campaign committees can be huge. There can be thousands of people working for each candidate. These people may live all over the country. They help voters learn more about their candidate.

Serving on Committees

You might have been on a committee. If you've worked on a project with other students, then that was a committee. Committees are groups of people who have the same goal.

Volunteers

Candidates have to learn how to reach voters. This process can take years. How can candidates know what voters want and need? They can do what Katy did. They can ask.

It would take too long to ask each person what they want and need. There are millions of voters. They are spread out all over the country. Candidates need help to win elections. This is where volunteers come in!

These volunteers support Abraham Lincoln in the 1860 election.

Each candidate for president may have thousands of volunteers on their campaign committee. These people meet voters who live near them. Volunteers ask voters what they want or need in a leader. Then, they tell the candidates what voters are saying. This helps candidates know what they should work on.

Volunteers help candidates connect with people. They also tell voters how their candidates can help.

Kamala Harris meets with supporters in Iowa.

Political Parties

A few months before a presidential election, the race heats up. The major **political parties** pick their nominees. The parties' nominees are who the party members want to be president.

There are two major political parties in the United States. They are the Democratic and the Republican Parties. They choose their nominees the same way. Party members talk and argue over who they think is the best choice. They vote in primary elections. Then, representatives from each state go to a convention and share how their state voted. After the votes are counted, the party announces the winner. People celebrate when this happens. They drop balloons. They wave signs and cheer. The nominees go onstage. This is the first time they are called the "nominee for president." It is a great moment for them!

Different Times, Different Measures

During the 2020 elections, the conventions were quite different. A world-wide health issue made it unwise for large groups to gather. Party members met online. Some gathered in their cars in large parking lots while the candidate spoke from a stage. Many people celebrated from their own homes.

Think and Talk

What does it mean to be a nominee?

The Democratic Party names Bill Clinton as its nominee in 1992.

Debates

After the conventions, one person represents each major political party's choice for president. The next big events are the general election **debates**. During debates, nominees meet onstage in front of moderators. The moderators' job is to ask nominees questions and keep nominees on topic. Moderators make sure debates are fair and focused.

During a debate, the candidates take turns speaking. They might decide who goes first by flipping a coin. The moderator may ask a question that the first person answers. Then the next candidate may have a chance to reply. The next question will begin with the loser of the coin toss while the winner of the toss replies. The debate goes on this way for a few hours.

About one in four people in the United States watch the debates live. The debates often play a key role in helping voters choose between the nominees.

Barack Obama and John McCain answer questions during a 2008 general election debate.

JFK vs. Nixon

The first televised debate took place between John F. Kennedy and Richard Nixon. Nixon was ahead in the **polls** but was tired and sick during the debate. Kennedy was rested and wore makeup. One-third of Americans watched the debate live. They saw how bad Nixon looked, and Kennedy moved ahead in the polls.

Election Day

At last, it is time to vote. Voters have studied the nominees to be able to make good decisions. It is time for voters to choose who they think will do the best job. That person will be the next president.

Some people vote in person. Other voters mail in their **ballots**. The votes are counted, and the winner is announced to the public. Some people celebrate that their nominee has won. Other people are sad that their choice did not win. It is an emotional time for lots of people.

Voters wait in line on Election Day.

Ronald Reagan takes office in January 1981.

Presidents take office in the January after they have been elected. They give an important speech. They tell the country what they want to do as president. But one person can't change things alone. So, the president will need help. Many times, people from the campaign committee go with the president to the White House. They get to keep working on their ideas.

Two-Term Limit

Voters choose a president every four years. If the president has done a good job, voters may elect the president to serve another four years. This is called a second **term**. No president can serve more than two terms.

Staying Involved

Katy won her campaign. She asked questions and listened to voters. She shared her goals. The voters chose her.

Elections aren't always that simple. Presidential elections take a long time. They have a big impact on the nation.

If you find a candidate you like, ask if you can help their campaign. That is a great chance to learn more about the election process. It feels good helping someone you believe in. You trust they will work for the good of all. It can feel even better when the person you support gets elected!

Whether you volunteer or not, it is important to stay involved. Ask questions about people running for office. Decide which candidates you support. Learn more about important topics. One day, it will be your right and your privilege to vote in elections.

A Democratic nominee speaks to a crowd of supporters.

Glossary

appointed—chosen for an office or a job

ballots—sheets of paper or tickets that are used to vote in elections

campaign—a set of events for a particular purpose or common goal

candidates—people who run in elections

citizens—people who have legal rights in a country; members of a community

civic duty—a duty people have to serve society

debates—events where people share opinions on topics

elect—choose by voting for an office or position

federal—relating to the main or central government of a nation

office—a position or a job in government

political parties—groups of people who organize to direct or influence the government

polls—places where people vote during elections

representative democracy—a form of government in which people vote for their leaders

services—work done by groups that does not involve producing goods

slogans—words or phrases used by a group to attract attention

term—the length of time during which a person holds a political or an official office

Index

campaigns, 16–18, 21, 27–28

Clinton, Bill, 23

debates, 24–25

democracy, 15

Democratic Party, 22–23

Eisenhower, Dwight, 17

Harris, Kamala, 21

Kennedy, John F., 25

McCain, John, 24–25

Nixon, Richard, 25

nominees, 22–26, 29

Obama, Barack, 24–25

Reagan, Ronald, 27

Republican Party, 22

slogan, 17

term limit, 27

volunteers, 18, 20–21

Civics in Action

People who want to make changes can work for the government. Then, they may make an impact on the entire country! But first, they must get elected. Candidates must also have clear messages for voters. Some candidates have catchy slogans.

1. Learn about who is running for a local or school election.

2. Decide which candidate you would vote for.

3. Write a paper about your candidate to persuade other voters. Support your opinion with facts.

4. Create a slogan for the candidate.